OUR JOURNEY

Jennifer Johnson, Jericha Johnson, and Hailey Johnson

Copyrights

Published via Kindle Direct Publishing

Table of Contents

Our Journey

Children and adults alike have their own perspectives on life and its issues. In this book a step-mother and her step-daughters share their different views through poetry.

Dedications

This book is dedicated to the family who pushes us to achieve our dreams and helps us find solace and happiness. This is also dedicated to the two beautiful girls who helped create this book.

CHAPTER ONE The Step-Mother

Growing Up Too Fast

Just yesterday you had an impish smile and a wild imagination.
Just yesterday you knew of no evil, sadness, or perverseness.
You admired me with no argument and tried to copy me.
I held you in my arms and soaked up your purity and innocence.
I held you and felt your love...
Just yesterday you slept in my arms and reached for me in need and want.
Just yesterday I did all those little caring things for you.
Amazing how you've changed.
You begin to venture on your own.
You won't let me hold you or even be in your presence among friends.

You want to walk alone when before you held my hand.

I watch you search for self and your own meaning to life.

You turn away my help and grow beyond innocence.

Planting my kisses on your face is impossible.

I fight to let you go and let you grow.

Playtime has come to a close and tears secretly fill my eyes.

We begin to drift apart and our understandings change.

Just yesterday.

As The Evening Settles

When the moon appears and gives the evening glow.
When the birds bed down and the lightning bugs glow
The stars glimmer and the gentle breeze blows.
I gaze upon the sky.
There remains the answer to life's mysteries.
Answers which we cannot know.
To find a path in this life both good and satisfying
The crickets chirp and the frogs croak.
Every little thing here is a miracle.
Unique and beautiful.
I take the moment to enjoy their presence.
The breeze among the trees and bushes.
Time that ticks away at every breath.

Little Creature

This little creature soft and warm.
The slow breath and the beautiful heartbeat.
This little body with big glowing eyes.
This little creature that needs me so and loves me unconditionally.
The only one who wouldn't leave me or judge me.
The only one who is pure in intentions.
Her antics make me laugh.
Her face brings a smile.
Her forced cuddle makes me softer no matter what my mood.

The Oath

I made an oath onto myself.
Never shall I let another in life's path be consumed
by the same fears as I.
I shall pass on my words of wisdom.
I shall hope no one makes my mistakes.
I'll be there to console and comfort.
A vigilante against the unjust.
A force in another's fate.
The guardian of love and peace.
The advocate of innocence and peace. No matter
how it starts.
Every situation can end in a smile.

The Three of Us

The three of us...

We are a team.

We are in sync.

Love and protection is what we have.

Reassurance from our daily lives.

Support of each one's dreams.

A criticism of each one's faults.

Honesty in our harmony.

Shared joys and shared tears.

Shared frustrations and shared fears.

We do it all together.

A family indeed.

This Woman

This woman I admire.
She could hurt no one.
She will help everyone.
She goes above and beyond and expects nothing in return.
She is honest and true.
She is funny and sweet.
She makes me smile and my broken heartbeat.
She is my shoulder to cry on.
My best friend indeed.

Advice Dear Child

If I could tell my children, the best way to go
If they would take head and listen to what I had to say
I'd tell them to...
Dream big
Take your time
See the world
Don't let them have your tears
Face your fears
Be yourself
Try your best
Never forget creativity
Don't lose your imagination
Never let go of your passion
Don't let others tell you how to be
Express yourself
Enjoy yourself
Demand respect and give respect
Love everyone and judge no one
Love yourself before you love another

Anger Inside

I feel angry.
I feel frustrated.
Stuck in the middle with no control.
I try to fix it and it makes it worse.
I leave it alone and it will fester.
I feel guilt for being angry.
I feel angry because I cannot change it.
What is a person to do?
If I tell you how I feel there will be a fight.
If I say nothing the resentment builds
I try my best to ignore it all and let it go.
But the thoughts come creeping back in eventually.
I tend to analyze it all way too much.
But that is just my nature.

Days Gone By

Where did the days go?
When did life whisk me from child to adult?
When did I decide it was time to change?
It was just yesterday I was going to high school.
It was not long ago I was sewing wild oats.
Now I have a career and responsibility.
Now I have love and children.
When did I decide it was time to change?
It seems like I was just on my own struggling with bills.
It wasn't long ago when I was purchasing my first car on my own.
Now I own a house and brand-new car.
Now I have a college education.
When did I decide it was time to change?
From child to adult was in an instant.
From on my own to family seemed like overnight.

Goodbye Child

You've grown too fast for my liking.
Just overnight it seems like.
From pigtails and braids to sassy styles.
From light-up shoes to designer high tops.
From bunnies to black.
From cartoons to music videos.
From cooties to boys.
What will I ever do?
My child gone.
She knows it all and makes her own choices.
I hope I've done a good job and guided her well.
I hope she finds her place in this world.
How it's all changed.
From needing me to not wanting me.
From coloring books to essays.
From my lap to her room.
From bubbles to cell phones.
Where have you gone?

Inspired

Inspired by my love or by my child.
Triggered by joy and sadness.
Influenced by my mood.
Inspired by nature or a good storm.
Triggered by a wet kiss from a puppy or a smile from a stranger
Influenced by a simple gesture.
Inspiration is a funny thing.
It comes on a whim and leaves in a wisp.
I learn to hold the moment in my mind.
To put that moment into words.
Upon the pages of my notebook these words do play.

Step-Parent

The toughest job a person can experience.
With highs and lows and sudden extremes.
Working so much harder to earn their love and respect.
Always the scapegoat for their anger.
Always in the middle of both sides.
Hardest balancing act there is.
Love that grows in your heart.
This child not of your blood in which you would give the world.
This child not of your body in which you would give your soul.
This open ear always ready but not always accepted.
These open arms always s ready but often refused.
Bedtime stories and kisses one day
Then fights and hate for you the next.
It's not your fault they feel this way.
Extra love is always better.

CHAPTER TWO Step-Daughter

Hailey Johnson Age 12

DADS

Dads are fun sometimes angry

But they love you no matter what you do

That's the joy of dads

You beg and beg till they give in

Soon they do, that's the joy of DADS

STEP-MOMS

Step-moms will always be there for you

They're like another overprotective mom

They take you places to show their love

But all you want is to have fun with them

Now you know if you have a step-mom

They will always be there for you

SCHOOL

School is like a jail

It makes you feel trapped

Is that how you feel?

You can't get out, there's just no way

But still you hang your head just like yesterday

YOUR FLUFFY BUDDY

Dogs are playful and loud

They are cute and cuddly with great big eyes

Some have soft ears while some have ruff ones

Some are big, some are small

Lots are just full of love

Dogs can be sleepy, dogs can be fluffy

Some can even be to puffy

A few get in your face and lick your cheek

You act like you don't like it, but you really do

Because you love your dog as they love you

THE WAY I FEEL

I feel boxed in, like I can't open up

I don't know how to express

Can you tell me?

I don't know where to go or where to look

My story is like it's told from a book

I feel boxed in, like I can't open up

That's THE WAY I FEEL

FAMILY

Family is like a big hug

You just feel warm

Some are different, some are cruel

Some are just complete fools

But you learn to love them

Because they're FAMILY

SISTERS

Sisters can be mean

Sisters can be angry, but don't worry

If they love you they'll get over it

In about a day, you'll forgive them to

Now you know your sisters will be there for you

THE WONDER OF NATURE

Nature is sweet; it smells like new bloomed flowers

But sometimes I wonder of nature

Are there unicorns in a bush?

Or are there fairies in the trees?

Or are there frogs singing with bees?

That's THE WONDER OF NATURE

Remember

They are to remember.

Never to be forgotten.

The past years have been kept.

We are getting sick of trying.

Suddenly we are always crying.

Now we have to get stronger and depend on our future.

We have to hold on tight and slowly get through our lives.

We have to take the path on the broken road.

Just Me

As I wake up and get ready for school

I think to myself Hailey be strong

Then I walk down the stairs real steady

But I had no idea what imp doing wrong

My sister is grouchy and I'm scared for the school day

But my mind is just not there

I grab my backpack and head out the door as the rain sometimes pours

I get to school where my friends all wait

As I am starting iSTEP tests

I am a little late.

CHAPTER THREE – Step- Daughter

Jericha Johnson Age 15

I want you to tell me…

I want you to tell me life will get better

I want you to tell me it's okay to cry

I want you to tell me I don't ever have to steal again

I want you to tell me that I won't be like that.

I want you to tell me that it's not okay to cut

I want you to tell me once last time that life will get better

Life is Like a Black Rose

Life is like a black rose

It's like a black hole

It's like a grave

When life is like this you hurt yourself

When you hurt yourself you hurt other people

It hurts them when they see you doing it

When life becomes like a black rose don't hurt yourself like I did

Life: Life is Pointless

Life is pathetic Life is cruel

Life might not get any better

Life might become stressful

People are cruel

They try to change people

If they don't then they hate you

If they hate you they make up rumors

When they make up rumors people believe them

They make fun of you

Preps like to see you in pain

It's what they feed off of

If you show you are sad or depressed

They know what to say to you

Show that you are strong

And don't let them feed off of you

Me

Here I sit in a dark room

Listening to music

I wear black shirts and black makeup

People tell me to be happy

They tell me to smile

But if they knew my life they would understand

I'm as depressed ad a person at a funeral

People are cruel to me

They tell me to go cut myself

Some people even tell me to cut down

I feel like they want me dead

I feel like a black rose

So here again I sit in a dark room away from the world

Preps

Preps are so cruel.

They have to be perfect.

If they're not perfect they want to die.

If they don't make other people miserable

They feel weak and they hurt for other people.

They tell people they should fail

They tell them they could just die

But they don't know my life

They don't know what happened to me.

They don't know my life

So I wear black and hide in the shadows.

My life would be better

If preps and jocks were gone.

I hope they understand one day

What they did to me.

I hope they feel bad.

I hope they know

That I won't accept their apologies

If they even care to.

All The Same

Preps and jocks are all the same

They say cruel stuff to people

That have a hard enough life.

When people make fun of them

They get depressed.

They feed of off their depression

When they feed of depression they do it more

When they do it more people commit suicide

Some of the people probably done even care

Some of them stay the same

They like to hurt people.

Some say you're ugly

Some say don't cut across cut down.

That's when people want to die.

This is why so many people die

If you are a person

Who likes to hurt people

I hope you are happy

You might kill another.

Love

I love the way he laughs

I love the way he acts

I love the way you say you love me

I love how you say you will never hurt me

I love everything about you

I mean it to be true

When someone asks who I love

I'll say your name

I hope when someone asks you

You will say my name

Never

Never will I hurt you

Never will I cheat on you

Never will I say I hate you

Never will I say you are nothing

Never will I tell you I love someone else

I will say I love you

Want

I want to see you

I want to hear your voice

I want to hear you say it's okay

I want to see you tell me it's okay

I want to hear you say you mean every word you say

I want to see you tell me you say everything is true

I want to hear you say you love me

I want to see you tell me you love me

I want you to hear me say you are my everything

Is It True?

You say you love me

You say you won't hurt me

Is that really true?

Do you really mean those things?

Are you just saying these things?

Do you just want to hurt me?

You say you love me

But do you even mean it?

About The Author

Jennifer Johnson is from a small town in Indiana. She is a scuba diver, traveler, small time actress, step-mother of two, and career woman. Jennifer began writing at an early age and the passion has stuck with her since producing several single and collaborative publications. She has been locally nominated in the "Who's Who" of literary arts, is a member of the local Writer's Guild, and has been nominated in Indiana Emerging Authors. Jennifer's publications can be found on createspace.com, amazon.com, and her local bookstores.

Also by this author:

- Random Thoughts I & II
- One Mind's Words I & II
- Red Eyes
- In Too Deep

Made in the USA
Coppell, TX
20 October 2026

93449778R00027